UNDERSTANDING LIFE'S SECRETS

UNDERSTANDING LIFE'S SECRET:

THE WILL CONCEPT

CATHERINE ASHFORD

Gritt & Witt Publishing, London

Other Books by this author:

Non-Fiction

A Book of Hope and Inspiration:

If Only You Could Tell - **By Penny Hall.**

I Cried: I Know Why I did, The Woman That I Am - **By Selina Scott.**

ABC With A Difference: **By Selina Scott.**

The Healing Love- - An Infectious Thing - **By Catherine Ashford.**

The Otherside of Polygamy: My Perspective, Is it a Curse or a Cult? - **By Selina Scott.**

Unveiling Hidden Riches - The Truth, Be Bold and Make it Happen -**By Penny Hall**.

Voice of Reasoning: My Better Education - **By Catherine Ashford**

Fiction

A Horn in The Ground and Other Stories.

Stories From Afar

Bessy and the Moonshine Baby –

The Midnight Visitor of Culture and Other Stories

© **Copyright Catherine Ashford,** April 2021. All rights reserved. This book is sold subject to the condition that it shall not, by way of trade, or otherwise, be lent, re-sold, hired out, or otherwise circulated without the Publisher's prior consent in any form of binding or cover, other than that in which it is published and without a similar condition including this condition being imposed on the subsequent purchaser.

Published in UK by Gritt and Witt

ISBN: 978-1-874550-42-6 UK Price: £6.50

CONTENTS

Acknowledgement

I am a Christian believer; and if I am to be honest, for the past three decades of my life, I had never lived in total submission to the Lord. However, it came to a critical point in my life that made me realised that I have to submit to the word. I cannot live the way I was living. I need to increase my faith. What did I do? I turned to the Lord.

There was a day I was driving behind a bus and saw the advert of a healing service. I noted it down. At the time, I was suffering with a painful swollen arm. I managed to attend the service with my daughter and granddaughter; and when I got home my pain had gone, and I was relieved of my stress.

Since then, I started attending the church and became a member. It was whilst in that church I regained my faith. I attended Theological Training at Glory House Academy; and achieved a Diploma in Discipleship. I would like to honour The Glory House Church, London, UK; and the family of believers' who played a huge part in my development, that impacted my life in faith.

Thank you.

DEDICATION

To all God's children and those who care to build their spiritual wealth and the lives of children in society. I dedicate this book in the honour of you all.

To those who are working hard to be successful.

Do not forget to ask for help.

Remember when you are successful do not forget to help lift others up. This is God's Kingdom Wealth.

INTRODUCTION

Dear Reader,

My first thought is about God. We are to understand how He defines success; and how we can truly apply this to be successful in life. Ephesians 4:13 states, *'I can do all things through Christ that strengthens me.'* Meditate on these words daily.

How we manage our spiritual lives and the things that are entrusted to us is crucial. Such as special gifts that God gives to us as our passions. He gives us grace according to the measures of the gifts of Christ. According to Matthew, He gave some apostles, and some prophets, and some evangelists, and some pastors, and teachers. For the perfecting of the saints, for the work of the ministry, for the edifying of the body of Christ.

I will begin this book with this righteous quote:
'Seek ye first the kingdom of God, and his righteousness; and all these things shall be added unto you.' Matthew *6:33.*
What do we understand by this quote? To do this you have to have a good measure of faith. However, in today's world many would seek everything else

first, except God.

To understand the saying from my point of view is to look for him to find him, and when you do, look up to Him, because he told us not to worry about anything, such as our basic needs as explained in Matthew 6:25 in such as what we eat, drink, or wear. We are reminded of the birds, the animals, the grass and moreover we cannot add a single thing to what He has made. He already knows we need these things, and when we seek and find him all our needs shall be met.

Understanding this quote: when I say, do not seek anything for yourself first. It means, do not think of what you shall eat, drink or wear. The divine Father knows you need all these things as I have already explained above. So, are we following these words or are we just doing our own thing, and what we feel is right for us? We shall see later what this means to us in the world.

What I write here, is to educate, to teach, motivate, inspire, lifts up spirits and encourage people. It is to bless, heal and to dignify the mind of men and women. To have a purpose in life and speak positivity in your life always. I advise, if you want to know more of life's secret, start reading Matthew 5, 6, and 7. These chapters relates to the teaching of Christ. Mainly, when Jesus was teaching, it was all about practical advice for living in this earth and more importantly, he speaks in parables.

I do not want to be too biblical in this book, but to give a road map to healthy living by spirituality. In Matthew 5, we find the Beatitudes, which is part of the sermon on the mount. Matthew 6 is where the disciples asked Jesus to teach them how to pray, which most Christians know as 'The Lord's Prayer.' Matthew 7, is what is known as the Golden Rule. 'Judge not, that ye be not judged.' I also want to add that, you should always have a plan in mind if you want to be a success. I shall give a lead here with four of life's secrets mottos:

1. Have a dream, Plan, and work hard.
2. Be Confident.
3. Be Reliable, and
4. Be Honest.
Happy reading

Catherine Ashford, London, UK

CHAPTER 1
The process of the Truth about Life

The law of life is to believe. Have faith and hope. I would coin the words, 'to live you have to be.' That is to have a firm belief with creative thinking of your success in life. Think about what is it that you really want in life. You will have to be specific in your wish. We talk about 'Energy.'

ENERGY. It is having the will power to do anything. Without 'Will Power' you cannot find the energy or strength to do anything. The perseverance of going for what you want in a legal way until you achieve it; is the key to success. Did you get that? I repeat. *It is your perseverance of going for what you want, and the will power,* that becomes the key to success. This determination drives the power of your will to do anything. It should be easy when there is the drive; and the thing that motivates you, is the power within you.

A good wisdom and understanding are needed to grasp the full principle of life. This should be a simple process which any one can grasp. To enable the principle of life to work in a perfect way, it requires under-standing. You can only get this by asking for wisdom from the Divine infinite intelligence, which is the Holy Spirit. This enables the principle of life to manifest perfectly.

The brain is one of the most complicated and powerful organs in our body; and it drives every part of the human body. So, keep the brain active and alive. Exercise it, read widely to work it out, memorize something, let me say, at least seven items in a day, and try to remember what you have memorized. Above all read the Bible. It is a powerful tool to help us live. Potentially, this will extend its memory power. The brain helps you to get up and do things. If the brain is lazy it would not yield anything. Even to get out of bed you would not be able to do it.

Your brain moves you from A to B and gives you the ability to do anything that you want to do. It is in synch with other parts of the body to give us freedom and choice. So, we need to take care of our brain to get it to work for us perfectly. As you move around, be inspired by things around you. They are there to help us grow and expand our mind and memory of thoughts.

Whenever you come from outdoor; and sit down resting, it is good to bring the outside inside, and use the joy of wonder to inspire yourself into the versatility of the universe, and what is in it. Draw your conclusion; and get your feedback of what you have observed in this universal world of wonder. We are all here in this universe to live life.

Learn from what you see and meet from outdoors along the way. It does not matter what it is. It could be plants, animals, the figures, cars, transportation, trees, birds and the bees, insects, and flowers, all made this wonderful world beautiful and exciting.

It is beautiful to ponder upon; and that is not all, when you observe these things, it gives the will power of creation and creative thinking of all things good. Be inspired and be motivated. What you see is kept in the mind for a short while, but if you keep on doing the same thing repeatedly, what you see and learn gets memorialized in your memory file. This is a list file that stores important documents in the brain. We call this the subconscious mind. Some say spirit man.

The mind is wonderful; and is a fantastic photo copier that is located in the brain. It copies everything, and creates what it sees, whether you like it or not. It works overtime, even when sleeping. It expands it like a magnifier and is also a locator. This is why I would say to anyone, be careful of what you focus on.

Only focus on the good things that matters in life. This inner man as I would also call it, heals you while you sleep, for this reason ask for healing in prayers before bed.

I would also like to say that it is the willing helper that volunteer its services free. It is a dignified magnifier. It elaborates the objects in its space and in time.

CHAPTER 2

The Gift of Wisdom

When you are discouraged by words or thoughts, you need what I call the invisible helper. The spirit, which is God, at any point in time, will bring wisdom to you to discern anything. Things that you want to accomplish, so,

- Have a Goal,
- Have a Sensible list that you can work on. Many calls this a measurable goal.

This means that you can be able to work towards it and achieve it. With the gift of wisdom, we use it at all times. More importantly, use it in times that it is needed for when dealing with serious and important decision-making issues. This gift of wisdom is needed to discern right from wrong. Many will say, 'follow your heart.'

In this case, you will discern what has happened, to discourage you continuing what was in your heart's intentions. There are those who we call 'destiny spoilers' and can dismantle your vision. So, keep your decision close to your chest.

Keep focus and do not reveal anything to anyone. Always keep your work to yourself if you are not working with some people. Do not involve them. Not every opinion matter. Be courageous, and not let fear enter your heart. Fear brings delayed destiny, and obstacles; and it is very intimidating. Instead, be brave and turn fear around to faith, so you can change it to what you love.

The World is full of jealousy, negativity and evil. Never let opinion of some human influence your idea. When you think that your mind is being swayed, you would have to use the special gift. This is where the gift of wisdom comes in to give discernment to see the opposite.

Think fast 'on your feet' as they say, and

know that opinions are mostly there to confuse you. You are to learn to trust your intuitive sense to know what to do. You will now have to use your wisdom and continue to invoke your idea which you started before the distraction came in.

Have an organized plan to deal with your business. Be persistent. There are those people with different opinions than yours, who would ridicule or scorn you.

Do not go for cheap advice, but make sure to reach your decision quickly, and act on it. If there are any changes you want to make, do it slowly as you go.

Do not be swayed by others; this is why you should secretly keep your plan to yourself. You may have to think hard before you act and have confidence. Be confident and persistent; and stick to what your plan is to achieve your goal.

Above all associate yourself with the right people. Remember the four points of Life's secrets motto listed in my letter earlier in the introduction. Number two.

'Be confident.'

CHAPTER 3

The Energies of Life

Law of Attraction works

The Mechanism is *the energies of life*, which is in you, that enables you to,

a)   Learn from what has happened.

b)   Recognize what is going on, and work on it.
Then lastly, to this Law of Attraction is,

c)   The Joy of enormous wonder.

What you have called for is now ready to be delivered in a big way. Discern and select the purpose of Law of Attraction (LOA). In my view, this is there to empower us so that we can empower others. It is there so that we are provided for, so that we can provide for other people that are in our lives. We are to know that this is not about us alone. When we help other people, the blessing comes crashing down on us like showers, bringing the 'Joy of

Wonder.' This is what happens when you call for anything using the Law of attraction.

Focus on what works. Do not focus on negativity. Think number one of the Life's secret motto. 'Do not be lazy' and never talk about how disabled you are. Work on your personal growth that will elevate you. You are to be consistent in your idea.

We know that life moves so fast that it can take you to where you want to be if you work at it. Make a list. A genuine list of the important things that you want to achieve in your life. You are to go through that list daily, reading through it and seeing yourself achieved all of them. The infinite spirit will open up doors and new ideas for you. These are called goals.

As you achieve them you tick them. A caution on the list of goals that you set. All of them will not happen together. The most important ones will happen the quickest. This depends on how much thought you put on them. Make sure that you work on your affirmations daily, believe and you will see the wonderful things that will begin to happen to you.

Open your heart to new things, and new ideas; and be ready to receive what you have asked for. The most important thing is that you have to believe that you are worthy in life and you can achieve good things. Let us say you want these things:

1. A good Job.

2. A higher education; say a degree course.

3. Starting your own business.

4 Personal growth and development.

5. Community Work.

These are just few of the things you can write in a piece of paper and stick to your fridge, your wardrobe mirror or top of the television. If you are like me, you would want to write and become a paid author. Put it in a place where you can easily see it. Keep on looking at it; and meditate on them daily. Morning and evening, for as many days you are able to.

Align yourself with the divine Creator in what is true and possible. It would imprint in your subconscious mind, and printed in the screen of space ready to be delivered to you at

any time. Always be positive in all that you do. Get the keys to Success!
The Keys to Success are:

Ask, Believe, and Receive.

This is the process of faith and hope. Have you ever heard some people say these three things? Well, it is possible to get what you ask for. There is a process in this.

Which is the principle of the Law of Attraction.

After you ask, you are to believe that you already have what you asked for. Think on your goals, and what you have asked for. Your thoughts then became things.

Thoughts are things. Your thoughts can make you wealthy or poor. You are to change your mindset.

Use the I can, and I will concept. So, choose riches in life. You are to use the I can concept to build on your ability and keep developing in your ideas.

CHAPTER 4

Affirmations

This is how you do it: You are to repeat over and over again your affirmations. Think of the list you wrote and placed on the mirror or the fridge. Set your eyes on them, your goals that you set. Never accept negative thoughts. Cancel negative thoughts whenever they show up. When it comes to your mind, say quietly:

'I can and I will.' and then continue with your affirmation. Be a positive thinker to use all the resources that you have available.

Always be motivated and determined in your life to get your goals done. You are to take responsibility for your actions and your life. Be Thankful for understanding life's secret:

Above all the third and fourth motto: 'Be Reliable and Honest.'

It is unfair to be blaming other people for your failure, or when things go wrong. This attitude will not permit you to change, and do the things you want in life. Blame culture is debilitating; and one more thing. Stop complaining if you are.

You are to take responsibility and continue to do what is right. This is what successful people do.

They realized their mistakes, take on their responsibility; correct it and take the next step forward. Always have a positive energy to work on your project. To 'ask, believe and you will receive.'

Making Life GOALS

My goals. My first and foremost goal in life, was to:

- Own my own business.
- I wanted to write books.
- I wanted to be with people that matter in my life.
- I wanted to keep few friends.
- I wanted to spend less time on doing nothing.
- I wanted to spend more time writing. Lastly,
- I wanted to explore other business areas.

CHAPTER 5
The Gift of Discernment

This is the gift to ask for in life. It can help you figure out what you need to do when you meet with negative opposition. Your spirit will inform you how you would go about handling your idea; and the decision that would work for you.

The Reality: This is the truth in your mind-set. You would be able to see the reality and the truth of how to deal with your idea. Do not waver, do not ask anyone. Go ahead and do it. Just Do It. I remembered when I turned fifty years, I wanted to do something important for me; and that thing was to run the three-mile marathon. I pondered over It for several weeks. There was this inner feeling which many call the inner man that was pushing it. I only told my husband and he supported me. Then said, you want to do it, then 'Just Do It' and I did.

Sometimes, it is only for you to have the good

partner for encouragement.

Always plan and stick to your plan. Make only minor adjustments to benefit you. Yes, you and your cause. There are endless possibilities open to you; and you will find that you possess the confidence that you need to enable you to deal adequately with your idea; that which will enable you to reach your end goal.

Have a vivid imagination to create your reality, as much as possible. I do not mean dream. I mean, 'Think it. See it; and go for it.' If it is in your mind it is yours. So, you will have to go for it. Just go for it and do it.

One thing I took out of reading widely, is how others can influence people's thinking if you do not have that wisdom to discern reality. Look back into most of what you have done in life; and recall how many times you have had setbacks through the discouragements of other people these I have name for, (destiny spoilers).

As they say, 'opportunity lost can never be regained.' When you have the opportunity, do not waste time; use it, make your life better.

It would be okay to go for it.

If you are to be truthful the moment you start thinking about doing something productive, you will notice that it attracts some negative vibes in your mind, to not continue with your intentions. When you reveal this to people who are not of like mind, it gets worse.

This may attract an enormous bundle of negative vibes, which will send messages to your subconscious mind. You are to ignore this.

Let us say, you want to buy a house to rent and bring in income, or you want to start your own retail business, the moment you tell someone, you will be discouraged. They will tell you that it will fail; not even giving you the chance to start. You will also notice that every obstacle will be coming your way, such as refusal of loan. You will have to wait for some paperwork to go through, all that will make you wonder.

If you continue to do what you see is a good idea; immediately you will begin to doubt whether you are doing the right thing.

This is what those who practice the Law-of-Attraction calls, the Opposite Attracts.

Saying that, it means everything negative will appear in your presence once you begin to work on your intentions to achieve your desired goal.

Another example: Let us say you do an affirmation to become successful in business, or a wealthy entrepreneur and also be a healthy person. The moment you begin to work on your idea for your project, everything negative will appear in your presence to stop you. Some of what you will experience will be:

Lack of finance, and more Spending, things you have not budget for, your health will play up; and this will set your mind racing. You will then be asking yourself several questions, as to whether what you are embarking on for your project is the right thing.

This will be a very disturbing experience which would challenge your understanding of life's secret. It would almost make you want to rethink and want to give up your project. Then it will be the time for, fight or flight situation. Don't be discouraged.

CHAPTER 6

Will Power

The centralizing force to drive power is the 'energy' within us. It is the will power that energizes our everyday life to get up and go. It is the driving force. Therefore, you should focus your energy on what you seek to achieve.

You are to develop your will power, train your mind to work for you. Use your brain and mind properly to work well, so as to work at what you need. I am not a psychologist, but knowledge and education, teaches us life's experiences.

I want to turn my attention to using the Will Power in achieving good grades at school, college and at university. Even to achieve at work or in business.

Some people may say that those who do not achieve high grades in their exams are lacking the Will. So training is required. I would agree to that thought, for the reason that, one needs a great deal of self-determination to achieve anything. Will Power is important.

What is Will Power? It is the ability to control yourself. It is critical if you want to be successful in anything. Give yourself a challenge to go for the best. This is what I call the 'determinant spirit.' Go for it to pursue your career or job or business venture. Take time to do what it takes to get you to where you want to be. It could do you good to use the 'I CAN AND I WILL' Process.

The Bible word says: *'I can do all things through Christ which strengthens me.' Phil, 4:13.*

The Mind Power. The mind can also set limitation. This is when the thought translates things into reality.

Pay attention to how it works. What we sow into our mind that is what comes out. We hear people say, 'what you sow is what you reap.' When you sow good seeds, it will bring out good fruits. Our thoughts should always reflect all positive things; and that is what some people may call, 'Karma.'

The Mystery of Life. Change your thinking and change your life. Life changes anyway, so no matter what you do. Change always comes. They may be good, bad, and ugly or difficult; but however, the changes come, you have to handle it with grace. Life is not always smooth going, nor would be a bed of roses.

Now and again things happen, and how it happens sometimes we never know. Sometimes, it would be as if we have been sleep-walking into life's issues. It is how you handle change that matters. No matter what age we are at, changes can occur at any time. Handle it with care and guard your heart.

Life does not mix matters, or pick and choose on what or who change should come to. It will come anyway.

Change your mind and do something. There is so much to do in life. Try to do something different everyday it helps. You never know until you try to do something, then you will realize that when you try you can achieve anything. When you apply the **Law of Life**, it becomes a mystery. When you make effort to go for what you want to achieve, it will come closer to you. It is like gravity.

The fundamental laws that operates in this world is: anything you want is available when you go towards it. You want food you go and buy it.

Do not talk about negative things. When anything negative comes to mind, immediately counteract it as I explained earlier.

Even if other people say it, you should counteract it straight away there and then with positive words. No matter what they would say to you, do it quickly. There is something called negativity. When you encouraged negativity in your life, it will come to you always. You think positive and positive things will operate in your life. The Law of Life helps us with this. If you want to be successful you work hard towards your success and you will be successful.

You want poverty sit, and do nothing; poverty will come your way. You attract things in your life. The Divine Creator, the designer of our 'life fate' wants positive things for us. Anything that comes to us is from Him.

Whatever you attract comes to you because of free will nature. What you create is exactly what comes to you. So, do what you can to create good things. Visualize good things that you need. If you need a beautiful home, go ahead see it in your mind's eye and work on it. Fill it with furniture in your mind, and see yourself walk through the door. It is your home imagine you living in it. This is how you do it.

If you create wealth in your mind, it will come to you. You can create healthy success by your thinking, and you will be successful in what you aim for. Wonderful things can happen when you think and call for your needs.

Have positive attitude to everything in life. Take fear away from your life. Have confidence and think fearlessly. Always walk tall.

Give complements to people; and the same will be returned to you. To everything in this world, there are laws to get them to operate perfectly.

There is the 'law of love and hate,' and the 'law of peace and of confusion;' these are all laws that will work when you use them correctly or wrongly.

In all the things we do in life they are propelled by the 'law of life.' Life has its own ups and downs. So, we need to understand these secrets.

Sometimes, you will be up and other times you will be down. It is how you handle it that matters than anything else.

When things happen to people, they say, it is so unfair. Of course, some things are not fair. Life is not fair either, if you do not handle it with care. Things does not have to be fair. So do not look for fairness in life or unfairness, as life can be cruel to us to be kind. We really need to live life.

What is necessary is to work towards what life has to offer, which is sanity and the goodness of all things. When you are in a rot, try not to stay there too long.

The mindset.

Control the mind and keep repeating positive thing over and over again. So, go get what you want now. Make sure you work on it legally. Make it work. Put all your energy in it. Stand up and be counted.

Change your mind set. Fight for what you want; and fight harder. Life brings on us many challenges and so as opportunities. Go for it. Do whatever you are passionate about. Do not sit and wait to get anything for free.

Andrew Carnegie, the industrialist, believes in helping those who helps themselves and believes in people taking initiatives. He also believes in collaborative work. He was the world's richest man in his era. He was self-disciplined in his lifetime.

You are to be self-disciplined. Be in control of your mind. Keep the meditation of 'I can, and I will' going on, that which is your dream desire. Choose your path wisely. Every day we meet the challenges in life that tends to affect us, but always look beyond that and use your initiative to solve issues. Have a strong mind and patience, to overcome those challenges, by using the will of your mind power. Always renew your mind and spirit, it is life. Meditate on the good things that can help you live life, and act when necessary.

Enjoy this one life that you have. You can only live once and that is why you have to make good use of it and quick. Love your life and live it. Believe in yourself that you can do it.

Seek peace and hold on to it. Seek for peace in your life when you are working on your dreams. Talk to yourself about the peace you want. Shake off anything, or anyone that brings chaos in your life. It does not matter who that person may be or what it may be.

Take a small dose of them at a time. If it cost you to not pick up the phone to that person, let them leave you a message.

When the soul is ready and willing to deal with chaos, you would actually be *nudged to give a call back.*

 Do not feel guilty.

There are those who are (destiny helpers) placed in your life at some particular time for various good reasons, so you have to take notice of what each one is doing in your life, and what they bring.

When it is all done; and their work is completed, slowly all of them would be moved away to carry out their work somewhere else. When your life has been shaped, do not forget to involve those who can contribute to your wealth as no man is an island.

You would need people to work with you in your continuing wealth building. These are called the 'influencers.' Always strive for peace. Rest while you can. Take time to do things and make sure that the mind is on focus in your dream.

One thing I want to point out in manifesting the 'I Will and I Can' process; you will have to be active in going for it. You are to be highly motivated. Work hard at the process to get the reward of good work. When you get there, you will know, as things will begin to happen for you. It would be a wonderful thing for young people to be trained to use their will power.

Mental discipline, and self-discipline is required in anything we want to achieve. This brings self-respect for who you are and what you want to become in your life.

Motivation and Perseverance

When the mind is trained effectively, it will achieve much at a higher level. With strong will power you can achieve anything you want. It requires courage, faith, and enormous determination. Judging from the world stage, according to the scene in the universe.

Some young people today do not seem to have any 'WILL' to do much, and great things. Perhaps they need to be taught to use their mind power to work hard at school. Firstly, it appears that they find it hard to communicate. Most will not listen so that they would learn, and believes they know more than anyone else.

Their energy seems to be wasted on foolish deeds, with no faith in themselves to achieve higher heights, and greatness. So, people make excuses for them. This is wrong.

Neil Armstrong with his team had great Will Power; and so achieved the ambition of going into the moon in the 60s. For this man, failure was not an option, he and his team did it, and were successful.

Self-discipline. Be disciplined enough to persist in getting what you want, and to where you want to reach through the leadership, and guidance of the spirit in you, so, keep listening for directions. Your driving force behind the want, and your need is the discipline that you have.

Be Motivated.

Thrive for what you need before anything else. Do not dwell on wants. Find a road map which is in you. The Holy Spirit is the road map that sign posts and allows you to navigate your way to achieve your end goal.

Most people use other people to model their lives on, so that they can get to the point of where they want to be. There are others who will struggle, but it all depends on the motivation and self-determination.

Perseverance is also one of the key points to get you to the desired goal. For example, I wanted to pass my exams and the only way I could, is to study hard and focus on my end goal. Which is to get a degree.

I was taking my accounting examination when in the middle of the exams I started having tooth ache. I attended all the days that I was supposed to take the exam papers. I took pain killers to help me when needed. I never once say, 'I can't', of course, I cannot, is not in my vocabulary, 'that word is missing'. I was determined to take it.

I had pain killers that was in my bag; and had already took one before leaving home. Concentration was the hardest bit when you are in pain, but in spite of that, drive motivated me and I persevered.

I was not concentrating on the pain; but on my end goal; and when the results were out. I passed.

There would be some young people's eyes, that appear to be halfway shut towards their future. I pray that their eyes would be open wide, so that they wake up. I want the blame culture to stop, where anything that goes wrong in their lives is someone else's fault, or someone else's responsibility. It would serve well, if people open their eyes, and see the end goal of future achievement in life. Always have a purpose in life.

When you wake up in the morning, have something to live for. Even if you are taking care of a pet, that is something to wake up for each day, as you are looking forward to caring, and to do something for it.

Talking about young people in this context. It would appear that some of them has low motivational skills for themselves; nor do they have much desire to attain better and higher education.

The Will Power is not seen in them. Their eyes seem to be either shut or sleepy. There is no vision or wisdom to achieve and succeed in life. Such as the saying goes 'He who dares wins.' The children would have great future, peace, and harmony if they just try a little harder. I would like the young people to dare themselves to a better and higher future, by using the 'I Can, and I Will' process. If you want to be somebody, or anybody, you can, and you will.

Judging from what is going on in society, it does appear that there is no dare in the bones of most people. Could I use the word lazy? To me, this seem to be the case of the mind that needs to be trained.

I cannot see determination, confidence, hope nor the spirit of achieving in most of their lives. It seems as if their hope has fade.

I would hope and pray that they would raise their expectation of life, so that they begin to think positively to promote themselves into high achievers. I pray that the motivational thinking in this book can wake up the dead bones in lots of people. So, I pray for the youth of today. It should revive them so that they could achieve their full potentials in life. They should have an ambition and go for it. It is well.

To achieve the best in life, it is to have an ambition. In so doing, work on it. Begin developing the way to future living, so as to enjoy the best that there is. So, work on your Will Power. I know that the words and advice in this book will boost the lives of many and boost confidence; and enable self-motivation.

The feel-good factor always helps you to work towards your goal. Make a worthwhile decision now. Have a purpose.

Have a goal, and a determination for your future. This creates great imagination on how to get to your ambition. Aim higher to get what you want and work on it. I use this model below to keep in track:

- Good works, and
- Gestures that are good.

It pays with doing good to those who are in need. It is good to have a mentor. All things wealth comes from that. You are to follow your mentor's steps. Study how to become rich from your mentors if you have one.

If you have not got a mentor, make the effort to get one soon. You will experience the joy that it comes with.

I used these words daily to build up my energy: 'The Joy of the Lord is my strength.' Look at the push factor.

The Push Factor

Pull yourself Up, Step towards your goal and be Happy,

P – Pull yourself

U – Up

S - Step towards your goal and be.

H - Happy (PUSH)

So, 'Go for it.'

Your goals are going to push you.

Your dreams are going to push you to the limit.

The opportunities that are available to you, is going to push you to that higher heights. Your ambition will pull you up to where you should be.

Life's Purpose

Find your way to get to your purpose. Take the steps you will need to bring change into your life. Write down the steps that you will need to take to get there. Use your imagination to how you want your life to be. Here are some of the steps.

Write a personal statement that you will use

to work with. In business we call it:

Purpose or Plan.

1. What would you want your life to be like?
2. How would you like to get there?
3. What would you do to get there?
4. What is your life's purpose that would guide you to your goal?
5. How would you see yourself achieving it? Or what will stop you.

Write the answers to the above questions and take steps to work on them.

CHAPTER 7

Understanding life's Purpose

To understand the purposes of life is to start from your education. What is life's purpose? In my understanding, it is to live in this beautiful world that is created for us. To love the Lord with all our hearts, and our neighbour meaning the man you see walking in the street.

Apparently, love everybody with pure love as yourself.

Life's purpose is more than just living. There are other qualities that we should possess such as:

1. Having good conscience,

2. Knowing the difference between wrong and right, good, and bad,

3. Have the capacity to love purely,

4. Having the desire to see justice,

5. Having moral standing,

6. Having creative ability.

In understanding life, we are to have a good relationship with God. You are not to think about what you have. There are more important things in life than things. Traditional education is good, but also, skills that you have had to learn outside schooling, is also important.

Think about how you intend to use it for your purpose. With good relationship with the Lord, and keeping up with the special qualities that we are given, it will be well. Key to achieving wealth and success:

1. Have courage to go for what you want. You are a winner; and you were born to win.

2. Have moral values and qualities to be successful because this is what it is all about.

Here below are some clues to help you achieve your goal. Wait for this. Remember that thoughts are things.

The first thing that should be done is:
1. Change your mindset. When you

change your mindset, you will effectively be able to change your life. This is dealt with in chapter 6.

2. This means that you will have to change the way you think about everything you do.

3. Believing that you will be successful in your endeavours.

This belief leads to physical manifestation. Which is what you will experience.

Remember the 'I can, and I will' concept. Always think that you are worthy to be successful.

Have knowledge and understanding for the purpose that you are embarking on. The ambition to be successful will help you to focus on your wish and idea. It helps you to concentrate and build on the hard work that you have started.

Start building on your ability with enthusiasm, on what you know; and what you are able to do. Continue to develop on what you are doing. As you continue to work on your project you should see the end goal clearly approaching. See and imagine what your life will be like when you have achieved the desired goal.

Allow your imagination to work for you. It will almost appear like a daydream, but it is not. It is real to you, as your subconscious mind goes to work on your behalf. It will give you the strength and the energy, the drive to push, push; and push forward, so that it enables you to achieve your end goal quicker.

The enabler which is the spirit will keep pointing you to the things or tools that will help you to get to your destination. This is no joke. 'It works.'

Set your eyes on higher heights. Go for what you want. Proclaim it. The Prime Minister of the United Kingdom, Mr. Johnson from a young age, is said to aim higher to become 'world king' (credit The Guardian). Well, he did not become a world king; but he definitely is king in his own right. He won the general election with heavy majority members of Cabinet in 2019. I believe that, to be a Prime Minister is just the same as to be a king in his department as head of the sovereign country.

This is how you manifest going for something you want. During his career he had many positions that led him to where he is today, including becoming the London Mayor, and Hosted the 2012 Olympics. You too can do it if you set your eyes firmly on your idea and goal. Winning is the key word. Go for it to win and get to the top post.

To get to where you want to get to, use a signpost, and find those who are successful in your area of interest. Study their life patterns, and how they got to where they are. You would need to go on a fact-finding mission. Get all the information you need for your own interest in reaching your goal. It would not be easy because no success is easy. It needs hard work.

If you ask most successful people how they become successful they would have a long list of explanatory notes to show you how many bumps, hiccups, curves, and turns they went through. They may have been doing their business secretly and slowly for some years.

As we always hear the phrase saying: 'Rome was not built in a day.' So are that of many of the rich and successful businesses. This is why when I hear people say, meditate, shut your eyes, and call for what you want, and it will appear in days or weeks it grieves my soul. Nothing is that easy, and it is not true. If it is, it must be a one-off fluke.

Something had to be done to get to your wish. If you take time to find out how these people get to where they are, you will find the result astonishing. There may have been many turns, bumps, and twists. Many failures and disruptions. However, these people have self-discipline and determination to reach their end goal. In spite of all the obstacles, they kept going.

They know that failure is just a steppingstone to get to the point that they want to be. I call it a learning curve and others say feedback. All of them are correct. When you assess what they are doing, then you would understand. It is steering you in the right direction for your future achievement.

Now that you have known that you need a role model or a mentor you can chose the one that you believe is close to your aim and ambition. You can now begin to find out more about who you have chosen.

The best place to find good information of notable people is from the local library. You could use the social media and google them. Usually, you can get a short synopsis of your mentor/role model whichever way you want to call your chosen person.

From my point of view some of the information can be from the following medium:

Magazines, Books, their Biography, Video, Documentary, Films, You-Tube etc.

Find out as much as you can and read extensively about them. Such as their education, their mannerisms, their attitude, their character, their demeanour in public. How they interact with those around them. Find someone who can enable you to get to where you want to reach. It may be your very own Destiny Helper.

You would want to model your idea from your chosen person. One who will motivate, inspire, direct; and get you to function. You will be looking for the values, and ethics that this person hold, especially attitude and behaviour in society. What are their achievements, their educational and training attainment; and model their life for your purpose.

When searching for your role model go for high achievers. Find out about speeches that they have made. Interviews that they have done, and pay attention to the work they have done, also pay attention to what they are saying.

If they are writers, read their books to find out and learn how they got their stories so that you could learn how to get your information too. Observe their way of thinking, carry on and do not waste time. Take control and be calm in all you do.

Exercise, and breathe easy.

Meditate if you can.

Work on your self-discipline, and will power, which would be the knowledge, and skills you have so as to do what you want to do. Use your intuition, initiative; and imagination; and have a positive outlook on everything.

Always focus your attention on your wish, and what your end goal looks like; and how you are going to get there in life. In moving forward with your plan make effort to attend business conferences, meetings, and some free activities. Join business clubs so that you can network. You may be able to pick up tips on how to be...

Fearless

Fear brings delay and obstacles. There can be no happiness in your life when there is fear, anger, and jealousy. All that it might bring, perhaps is failure in life. To have faith is important, so that you can speak the word over your life; and it will be done. Do not be filled with fear and doubt. Trust in your faith. Faith is the rock of fearlessness. Have an Active faith.

'For God has not given us a spirit of fear, but of power, and of love and of sound mind.' *2 Timothy 1:7.*

Follow the principles in life; and you are on your way to success. You are to use the guiding principle for assurance, and for achieving financial wealth. Just like when you plant seeds in the soil, so you will have to sow the idea and your intensions in your subconscious mind. You are to know that there is always a divine plan for your life, waiting to be manifested.

Working on your idea

In your quest to deal with your idea of creating your wealth, you would have to believe in your idea, and command self-reliance. Never accept the fate of poverty.

Poverty is sickness. It is a disease that can ruin lives. It can kill. Walk tall; and look forward to your riches coming to you as you work hard towards it. Having development growth needs sensible goals.

What do you need goals for? Take a look at your career. This is what you do with career if you want to be successful in life. Goals are important in life.

CHAPTER 8

Career Goals

- What is your idea?
- Have you chosen your career; and do you know what you want to do?
- Look at what you want to do in life.
- Check the list you have made earlier, if you have one.
- Have a time scale; and how you want to achieve it.
- What will take you there, and what you will need?

Physical goals

- Keep your body fit and healthy.
- Watch your health and eat the right food to help you to concentrate on what you do.
- Keep your mind, body, and soul in good condition.
- Exercise and meditate when you can.
- Drink plenty of water it helps to wash, cleanse, and refresh your body system.
- Have plenty of rest.

Family goals.

Have time for your family. How you will work with them whilst you are developing your career. You will always need their help. What do you think that they can contribute to you getting to your end goal? Which will be your destination.

Spiritual goals

Everybody needs spirituality in their life, and I suppose you would need to set a goal for this too.

Time for praying.

Do you aim to achieve a prayerful life? Keep on praying.

Meditate daily? Set a goal how you intend doing this.

Friendship goals

This is also important as with family. This is a big think.

Think on the following and work on them: How many friends do you have in your life?

What are their purpose and benefits to you, and also to them?

What time do you reserve for them?

What do you do when you meet them? Have a clear goal for this, as time is essential whilst working on your career.

You may not have plenty of time to do all what you aim to do, but you would have to include them at some point to enrich your life.

Intellectual goals.

How far do you want to reach with this career?

Do you want to go into politics? Or Do you

want to develop your career further into re-search in human behaviour, or government? Set your goals on this. I was a social worker; but I was hugely political and critical in the way the government operates. So, I set up an organization to contribute to society.

Social goals

Are you a member of any organization?

Set your goal on how many you could join and have the time to attend meetings to par-ticipate in policy making and development. Functions that you will have to attend, train-ing, conferences, seminars and socializing with friends. Attending social functions all has to be thought of, and put into perspec-tives on your way to success. However, never lose sight of your goal, and where you are heading to.

CHAPTER 9

Observations of the young

Do not get me wrong. As a social worker, by biggest concern is how to deliver for these young people, to make it work for them?

I have worked in every area in the community and watched with interest; and in amazement, seeing how some young people sit in a state of dependency. They want anything; and everything for free. Not making effort to give back something to society is astonishing. Not even to care for themselves. It appears to me to be a non-spirited effort; and I believe that some motivation and self-discipline is needed, as well as dealing with their mental wellbeing. Being that it does not appear to be the right way to live life harmoniously, where many has underlying issues.

It is always good to give what you can to the universe, and it will give back more than you expect. Let those who are strong help the weak, carry them with you and pray. Coming back to where I left off about the Law of Attraction in chapter three, as mentioned of how it operates.

After you meet with negative set back to your plan, you should be strong, as you would have collected some ideas from your mentor; and now ready to put them into practice at this point. You should never give up. Do not look back, you will only see obstacles when you remove your eyes from your goal. Have the desire to achieve that which you set out to get.

Think back at what your idea was. What was the aim in the first place? **Your goal,** this is what will motivate you. (Impossible to get there will never be your language) Always focus on your goal and the destination you seem to be moving towards.

It is important to remember that all things are possible to him that believes.

Reach for your destination and set your heart on your goal. Where are you going, and where do you want to be?

Do not listen to any criticism; and do not

allow it in your life to stop your challenges. These are all stepping-stones to get you to where you want to be.

Always keep your eyes on the goal. Your wish, and your goal will soon become fruitful. So now, go back and look at what you set out to do, and begin to work on your idea.

Manifestation. Here is an example. Many people do not believe that Law of Attraction always work. How it works, is not fully understood. But Hebrews 11:10 explains this clearly in faith. Saying, 'For he looked for a city which hath foundations, whose builder and maker is God.' So we are to operate by faith.

I was manifesting to get something done with my home. As soon as I started, my attention was turned on to some of my family members, who were poor; and living in a life-threatening condition. Like in a squalor. I had to stop what I was doing and went to their aid. Do watch out for these distractions, though it is necessary, because the Law of Attraction demands it. It can slow your process. So, it is important that you know what to do. What to do is to go back to the beginning of your manifestation.

My Story

As I was in the middle of dealing with my goal, something personal was revealed to me to do with family matters. This means, the revelation of the personal matters was to do with family, require my utmost support. It requires lots of money to be spent.

Now my attention is turned to that project which requires lots of spending of the money that I was saving for my project. That was not all, as I was dealing with the project at hand, there were other people from the family who kept coming to ask for help and demanding money.

It was like a big mess, and I was thinking, and asking; did I get anything wrong? No. This is what should happen as you should be of service to others. The home I was building for the needy was completed; and I then went on to arrange the wedding of my nephew from start to finish. Now, always have in mind that whatever you give out comes back in abundance.

This is the *opposite of the law of attraction.*

Everything kept coming in a powerful way to throw my mind off my original plan, which is to manifest my business project.

You are to concentrate on what you are doing, as I have stated several times earlier in this book. Do not let these distractions or anything else interfere with your work.

This is a classic example of 'The Law of Attraction,' which says:

The opposite attracts. It works, as it was a testament to the happenings.

The critical moment

I want to do something positive for myself, when suddenly, the negative stuff appears. Though helping others is not negative idea, but many would view it as negative to what you want to do, since it was an obvious distraction.

This example is a lesson that we should all endeavour to learn. I have mentioned earlier that you should not be sharing your idea with anyone. You can share with the partner who is part of the process to get to your perceived goal; and is part of the process, that is, if you are on the same mindset.

Strong Will Power achieves great things and accomplishes goals. You can share your method when you have achieved your goal to help others.

Become a mentor yourself for others, to help them get from A to B. Doing this will help you grow in your walk to destination goal. The reason not to share in the beginning of your project, is that you will be discouraged by those who do not want you to be successful.

People can be indifference to your thinking, though we know that they do not have the power to affect your plan; but their comment on your method could be negative.

Also, you are to be aware that there are those who would try to stop you with negative intentions. They appear to have no positive direction or good advice to give. They may be the destiny spoilers. Do not affirm their saying. Words have power, speak positivity on it. Do not sow negativity in your life.

Remember not to sell yourself short of your

blessing.

The Law of Opposite creates negative experiences. Which is the opposite of what you are seeking. This is when you should use the gift of Wisdom. As explained earlier. You will have discernment to enable you to work on the idea that you have in the first instance.

You have to go back to your initial idea and move swiftly with clarity. This will be that which you were working on to get to the destination. It would do you well if you pray about the situation to reveal to you what is the truth. The happenings, and how to handle the situation will be revealed. You should see. things for what they are now clearly; that it is brought on by a force that is more powerful than you; so as not to fall into the hands of negativity.

There are many people who have businesses who had met with setbacks in their lives. I learned that they persevered and worked through it with courage. It is a learning curve. Courage is what will enable you to go on.

I want to assure you that every failure is a

lesson, and a feedback. It is an opportunity to learn and move on to the next level. This is where you can correct any mistakes that has been made on your way to success.

When you fall, you are expected to be able to get up again and walk. If by default, you are not able to get up immediately by yourself, there are sometimes good Samaritans to give you a helping hand to get up and go. Turn to your mentor and ask for advice or go back and study what they did when things work out in the way that they did not intend it to go.

The divine spirit does this for us automatically because he lives within us in our body as its temple.

When you know this, you will have the encouragement and the push to continue. I want you to be encouraged as you read this book. You will be inspired; and above all you will be educated and encouraged. Therefore, if you fail in a project, keep going and the success is somewhere down the line.

Failure is not an option. So, go for the success for wealth. It may be long or may be short;

but you will eventually get there, no matter what. Only believe. You will either do it by yourself, or someone will help you along the way.

Do not let anything stop your dream. Keep working on your intentions. As long as you have life and good health, there is hope.

When you stumble. Try to recognize the problem, and work on it swiftly to change things. Educating yourself; the mistakes made are important; and is part of life's lessons.

When I met with a wall whilst trying to help family. I was told to stop but I did not. I prayed for wisdom to help me. It is up to us to figure out good and sensible advice, whether it suits our understanding of the project at hand, or on a spiritual level. Failure is not negative. It is an opportunity to improve and move on to a higher level of wisdom. I say it is a lesson in disguise that can be turned into an opportunity.

I keep saying that failure is not a bad thing because I know it. It is a lesson you learn from what is thought to be negative. In a sense it can actually be your reality, and of course it is a positive thing. We now have; wisdom and understanding in next chapter.

CHAPTER 10

Wisdom and Understanding

Life can work better for us when used properly with the infinite intelligence. The subconscious mind will propel your desire to the goal.

The Law of Attraction, seeks to empower you on your journey in life with the spirit as life's pointer, or map, so that you can prosper. See below what the wisdom says about life.

The Truth of Wisdom I am reminded of two areas in living life.

Spirituality and Faith.

Just imagine if you could have the insight to look into your brain right now; and see how it connects with your mind to work perfectly for you. It would be a great observation. Just seeing how the two interact perfectly for your purpose:

- To heal, to protect, and to provide.

Always make a point of having a quiet day to look back into your life; and see through what is happening in your walk to destiny. This gives you the opportunity for hope. Hope, in this I believe drives your energy and strength to enable a hope for a brighter future.

Imagine when you have the opportunity to work on all of the negatives; and turn them into positives, what a joy it will be. That signifies the truth of your wisdom and the truth of life.

More importantly, there is more to life other than us being just in existence. There are also plenty to live for than just things. The structure that drives the attitude is the wisdom of motivational force, that directs you to your destination.

CHAPTER 11

The Principles of Life

Have patience in Life. Some say that the best way to live life is living life that is worth remembering in the future. The most important Principle of Life is 'Patience;' and the Law of Attraction requires this.

WILL POWER

The centralizing force is the energy within us. It is the Will Power that energizes our everyday life. Therefore, you should focus your energy on what you seek to achieve. You are to develop your Will Power and train your mind to work for you.

Concentrate on the positives with generous portions of faith, patience, and determination.

I have explained the brain and mind earlier of how to work at it, so that they work for us.

If you want, you can turn your attention to using the Will Power in achieving good grades at school or at college and at university.

Step boldly and consciously into your train journey to your future life.

It is possible, just follow the explanations here:

- Be persistent.
- Be vigilant at everything you do; above all please,
- Be nice and kind.

Life on its own is a cycle. It goes around and encourages us to experience living life; and all that there is in the universe.

We are to know how to live with love, in peace, and in harmony with others; and with ourselves.

Life is always ours to start a story and to end it with a beautiful swirl of love. We start our life's story when we are born. So, every day, we add a little, and another day, we add a little bit more, until the final story is told. Then life becomes interesting as we move around in the universe.

We may think we have more to life in living. But everything we do is to enable us to experience and accomplish all that we need before reaching the end of the swirl.

Living in this world is for ourselves, others, and also for the divine Creator; so that we live in perfect peace and harmony. We are to help and support others with our services.

We are to care for each other, in some way. Thus it makes for a better community.

The divine spirit intends for our life to be this way. When you are in a position to help others, do so selflessly without any motives, and with all good intentions. This will bring all good things that you desire to you; and your light will shine through, and so you will be counting your blessings.

Patience is the element of the Law of Attraction, as I mentioned earlier. We must be patient to do what we are doing, to enable us and empower ourselves; and also to empower others.

I have dealt with **the Law of Wisdom** earlier which confirms and suggests that wisdom should always prevail in anything we do.

Sometimes with discernment we can do it as directed by the good spirit in us. We should not wait for someone to direct us. We would be able to work towards our goals, taking the initiative. This means to do what we feel is right, and what is our gut feeling in the situation we have in front of us, so as the spirit leads us.

The last and final decision is with us by the spirit, which is the divine love that comes with inspiration and guidance to help us work on our project. It directs us right through with it.

The purpose of the Law of Attraction is to allow life to preserve itself within us, with strength and in the utmost extraordinary and magnificent way; and in the lives of those we support and also for us. I shall give an example of manifestation at work here.

This is my second story:

This is more like a testimony. When you give it comes back to you three-fold. So, it goes that I was always giving food stuffs to charity in supermarkets whenever I go grocery shopping. When I shop for my home, I shop an extra bag for charity trolley too.

I had been doing this for over fifteen years, since I find myself back into the life of faith and spirit filled believing. I never knew that one day I would be receiving that same charity when it is so needed in a time of want.

In 2020, the world was fighting an invisible war. This war is the Corona Virus, scientifically named COVID-19. A potentially killer disease was so real. Everyone was forced into an induced fear by COVID-19. For some genuine reasons I was not able to go out to shop for groceries.

Having underlying health concerns, I was classed as vulnerable group person. So, I should be Shielded from the disease. I was not to go out, nor anyone from my house. I could not go out to get my weekly shopping. Neither was I able to shop on-line, and so I was running low on food.

I was now getting worried and thinking of what to do when once the last food in my fridge is finished. As they say the rest is history. It was the Law of Attraction working on my behalf this time. It was my history of giving hope to others that was working for me, and led by my usual habit of providing for the needy. I was now in a position of need. I sat down praying, lamenting; and hoping that I shall be able to buy food on-line soon before I starve.

The story now concludes when I received a phone call informing me of help that is available to me from the local authority, through their community scheme, 'help for the needy.' I was qualified for that help. So, I was informed when the help for me would start. It so happened that it came just in time, before my last lots of food disappeared off the shelves and the fridge. How appropriate that my support for the needy was paid in a strange way that I was not expecting.

This is the reason why it is good to share and help others.

I believe that I probably have received more help than I had been giving out to charity. This is the understanding of Life's Secret when we work with the Law of Attraction.

The mechanism of manifestation

This manifestation would work perfectly if

used properly. It is there to provide for all other people in our lives; and for all those whose life we touched with our services daily.

You are to use the Law of Attraction to bring all those things which you want for yourself into the lives of others. Those services could mean, to give help to the poor, feed the hungry, the homeless; and all those that influences our lives. This is when we would see all good things manifesting in our lives.

The Energy of Attraction:

This means that we should seek first the kingdom of God; and all these things that we provide for others would be added unto us. This is when we would see the multiplication of the Energy of the Law of Attraction.

When you are in wealth, help others to be in wealth too. The more you give, the more you get, as people say. Always accept gifts, however small, it is your blessing; and the will of the spirit will also bless the giver. The divine spirit will be in your favour.

The words are:

'Ask and believe' and it will be done.

Be gracious and thankful for everything all of the time.

The next subject in this book is about working towards your wealth and manifesting your needs.

Again, this is important to keep in mind. 'Patience' is the key when manifesting wealth. The Principle of Life requires zit. There are lots of books written to this effect. Blogs, and videos talking about the realism of how to get rich; and earn millions with law of attraction by using metaphysics are all in the market.

The most popular book in the eighties and nineties was the 'Think and Grow Rich' by Napoleon. I happened to have two of the same book. My daughter bought me one, and I bought the other one, when I could not find the one that she bought me. I like packing things away, and as an avid reader there are lots of books, and some that I cannot find myself to read quickly.

Sometimes, as we all may agree there are other things that takes priority in life. So, the book was packed somewhere beyond my reach.

Thank goodness, I have both of them now; and had managed to read it right through. I also read, Rich Dad, Poor Dad. All these books fed my spirit and gave me a lot of comfort, to know that I was doing the right thing to acquire my wealth.

It changed my behaviour completely. The way I speak, the way I respond to questions; and the overall way of doing things in everyday life. They were food for thought and medicine for my health and wealth.

Though I took a lot of ideas of how to create wealth, there was not a clear cut on exactly how to go about doing it when I watched the movie, 'The Secret.'

This film showed us many of the people in it talking about what they have manifested and the next minute these things are on their door. Well, no one should take that for the gospel truth. To me all seem like a joke.

However, the truth in that is, anyone has the power to ask for anything and receive it. They are not lying; it is the truth, according to the Book of Law.

The Bible word said, we are to ask for anything with faith, and it will be done. So, there are three main things you need to do, which are: Ask, believe, and receive.

This I have mentioned, once, twice, or more times above in previous chapters. You have to know who you are, and where you want to go. So be courageous, patient, and keep on going to achieve your goal.

Learn to be fearless in all you do; and take the bold step towards achieving anything that you want in life, so you can live a life of content with your wealth. You will know that anything is possible.

CHAPTER 12

Manifestation for your needs

However, anyone can use the manifestation technique. It does not matter what faith you have, whether you are a Christian, or any other denomination. 'It Works.' All that is needed is strong faith.

I have been manifesting for what I want and what has come to me is what is due to me. Anyone who want to go down the route of manifesting for wealth would have to exercise patience.

Waiting is the most important element in the process as with **Patience**, to receiving the wealth you need. There are ways to manifest wealth itself; and this is carried out by our thoughts, mind, and the subconscious state. It appears that it is simple to do though it involves hard work.

I take this opportunity to explain about what to do here. I would advise you to read widely on this subject area. The more books you read the more you are educated of life's principles.

More importantly if you can, read the Bible, there is a lot of life's information in it.

Many things are acted on according to divine principles and the law of life, which is to believe and wait. Have a firm belief and a creative thinking of your success in what you really want in life.

Health, Wealth and Peace
You can bring everything into existence by creative thoughts. This can be done in a repetitive manner. It is wise not to go astray from your thoughts. If you do, go back to where you started to manifest and start all over again. When this is done the subconscious mind picks it up and expands it; or better still amplify it and goes to work to bring you what you have called for yourself.

You will have to direct all things positively. I would say that you are to let your strength and determination led you to your wealth.

To begin with, you will have to renew your mind, body, and soul. Ask for the power of the infinite spirit to restore you. Open your mind to change; and to receive the abundance of wealth, which is health, harmony, peace, joy, beauty, happiness, love, and finance. This is what we call prosperity.

We are to love all, which is the fulfilment of the universal law of the Creator who gives us every good gifts that we receive.

The Mirror Image technique
The law of the mind is to uplift your spirit every day. This should be done with kind words and beautiful thoughts to yourself. Using the mirror. I will list some words later. Avoid negative utterances by immediately cancelling them with positives.

Make a point of saying these words daily. You can manifest anything by using the mirror. Create your own future with the mirror.
Manifest your wealth, money, or good health. Whatever you think in your heart you can achieve it. The technique is to create a feeling for your affirmation. Let's go…

1. Stand in front of the mirror and make sure you see from your waist upwards.

2. Make sure you are in a relaxed mood; and

your mind is clear and free from any clutter.

3. It is important to do this in the morning when you are alert after the night's rest.

4. Take a deep breath in and out to keep you relaxed.

5. You are to do this breathing in and out, three to four times. Before you begin to say your ideas and thoughts.

The action and the Art of Manifesting. Look into the mirror, firmly and straight into your eyes. Take a deep breath in and out, up to four times. Now relax as you are looking into your eyes throughout the mirror. Keep going. Say:

(calling your name, example 'Marian' then say)

- I love you dearly,
- I am a child of the Divine Creator.
- The divine peace fills my soul and saturates my mind.
- God guides, inspires and prospers me.
- I am beautiful.
- I know that I deserve the best.
- I am strong.

- I am special.
- I can do anything. Through the Spirit of the Lord.
- I am motivated to do well in all my being, and to achieve my goal and get to my destiny.

Write the above meditation lines in a piece of paper and meditate on it so you can say it without looking at the book and concentrate fully. You are to say the truth about who you are. Say how much you love yourself whilst manifesting.

It is by constant repetition you can send the message; and imprint it into the subconscious mind that will amplify your thoughts. Talk about what you want in life. Continue to talk to yourself; and talk about what you deserve in life. Other ways you can meditate is by following these statements below:

You are to say that you know that you and God are one. He lives within your heart.

Talk about your wealth and richness, and that you are rich in everything.

The divine spirit lives in your body. Say these statements over and over again; and feel the riches that is in your life. Write them on a piece of paper and stick them beside your bedroom mirror. Look at them and recite all of them always. Make your dreams come true as it is supposed to be.

To have peace and be happy,

Keep saying the words,

'The joy of the Lord is my strength.'

This helps a lot, and it gives a clear mind and inner peace. Also, in the mornings you can say,
 'This is the day that the Lord has made, I will rejoice and be glad in it.'

This is a good thing for the mind daily. It brings peace, bravery, and happiness throughout the day. It does clear the mind of all garbage picked up along the way; and helps you to live your life in peace. It brings contentment and good thinking.

These sayings are written in the Bible. They are not idle or foolish words. They carry the truth and will obviously impact soul and spirit.

CHAPTER 13

Gratitude

Give thanks every morning for everything to the divine glory.

Be thankful that you have seen another day.

Be Thankful that you have two complete hands and legs, think about those who do not have any, or have missing limbs.

Be Thankful for your eyes that you can see, there are lots of people who crave to have twenty/twenty vision and do not have them.

Be Thankful that you are in your correct mind. There are those who cannot think clearly.

Be Thankful that your heart is in the right

place.

Be Thankful that when you make mistakes you are able to correct them and move on to the right thing.

Be Thankful to the divine for grace and mercy.

Be Thankful to the divine for wisdom and understanding.

Be Thankful to the divine for the good times and the bad times.

Be thankful to the divine for love and forgiveness.

Be Thankful to the divine for peace, joy and happiness.

Be Thankful to the divine for health, healing, and wealth.

Be Thankful to the divine for kindness.

Be Thankful to the divine for sharing and caring.

Be Thankful to the divine for hope.

Be Thankful to the divine for differences.

Be Thankful to the divine for the fruits of the holy spirit.

Be Thankful to the divine for faith and patience.

Be Thankful to the divine for prosperity and blessings.

Be Thankful to the divine for beauty, strength, and courage for without them, you would not be able to be where you are when hard times meet you.

So, be grateful at all times for everything.

You should look at courage as a gracious attribute to life. With courage you will fight everything that comes your way, with might and strength.

You have to fight spiritual battles and barriers that comes your way. I am so thankful for everything. Every little thing that is spared to me I say thank you.

I say thank you for the good things, and also when there are bad things, I think of the good things and appreciate them more and say thank you all the same.

The information here are honest lessons in life. It helps us to grow and become stronger. I say that I am so grateful when I experience bad times. It made me appreciate what I use to have, and what I missed.

My reason for being so grateful is that I was taught to be grateful for every little thing from a young age.

One family member would take back what he has given to you because you did not say thank you. Which means that you did not deserve it and so you are not grateful. The more you show gratitude the more you become prosperous, and more will be added to what you have.

I once had a manager who would give you tip most times for hard work. If you complain that it was small; he would say 'give it to me so that I increase it.' If you do, he will take it from you and say, now, you forfeit all. He then added, 'let this be a lesson to you, that you should take what you have until you get what you want. So be grateful and say thank you.'

When you are asking for something, in a spiritual line, learn how to say thank you before you even receive it. Know that it is yours already, so be thankful for it. Thank the divine for all your blessings that took you to the point at which you are at the moment.

Not many people get to the point at which you are. Many fell by the wayside.

Say thank you for when you make mistakes you are able to correct them and when you fell you are able to get up. Say thank you always.

In my life, I say thank you to the divine creator, for all those who came into my life during the good times and the bad times. I say thank you for those who came for a short while and those who stayed with me all the way. Thank the divine for those who love you and those you love.

Those that do not love you and those that do not appreciate you. Thank everyone, right! You are to know that wealth is energy and flows freely everywhere. Call on your energy to flow through your body with divine love.

Divine order provides when you call on it. Having energy helps you to work on creating your wealth. Speak positive words in your life daily. This should be done in faith so that all good things will come to you. Doors will be opened in every angle to flourish your idea.

Gratitude means to place 'Thank You' in the top position to receiving anything. Saying, 'thank you' can open doors that have been shut to you. It can pave the way to your happiness, joys; and to your peace for greater things; and all that will come your way. If you want to prosper, this is it.

When you prosper, it means, you have everything, good health, wealth, money, peace, joy, happiness and many more.

Thanking the divine Creator, for everything is a sensible idea. *Thank you* is the answer to all our needs. I believe that it is a buzz word.

Always 'ask, and believe to receive.' Then be grateful for receiving it. Now could you take a look at the birds in the air, the fish in the sea and the plants in the garden, they are all taken care of without any bother.

The air we breathe and the things we have, are all riches and are free. So, thank the divine Creator for all of these things. We did not ask for them but were given to us freely.

Read the book of *Matthew chapter 25,* in the Bible. You should look at wealth as your best friend. If you have money, it is good. Money is good, and everybody should have respect for it; and know how to use it wisely when you come into it.

Money is divine wealth and belong to the Divine Master. Look after it with interest and stay blessed. **Money** is God's idea for everybody to have money and to be self-sufficient. If you have money; you can spend it on things you need in life. You should have good clothes, and eat good food and have decent place to live in.

The people close to you, the friends that you keep are all good things that wealth brings. So, thank the divine for all these things. Always say to yourself that you have abundance of wealth. The divine provides for us, inspires, and guides us to how we can acquire wealth and to live well. All these things are wealth:

To be able to see is wealth.

To be able to walk without aid is wealth,

To be able to eat unaided is wealth; and All good things that will come to you are wealth in abundance.

So, Thank you, divine Creator. **Money** flows when you respect it. Use it wisely and productively and it will flow freely as you request it.

To be able to look after money is wisdom; and *the law of Life* requires it. Spend money wisely and carefully, it is a divine supply by grace. If you do not look after the money and wealth that you are given, what you have can be taken away from you and given to those who can look after it by divine blessing. This is part of Life's Secret.

Money comes from the intelligence of the Divine Creator. It is a divine substance. Therefore, we should look after our wealth to enable more to be added to what we have. It is our divine right to have all things good. All things are possible to those who believe. You should think of **money** as the idea of Divine's wealth to help you living in abundance.

The Divine gave to the planet earth, the bees, the plants, the flowers; and all of the things we see in all our daily lives. It is to give us pleasure; and to enjoy them with grace and peace. We are to live in harmony with our neighbours, and in total happiness. Always care and give to others.

We are here to live a good life and to serve others as directed by the divine intelligence. We live by divine faith that helps us; and so, by this we can help others.

CHAPTER 14

Affirmations for Your Needs

Use these words to affirm your needs and you would be able to live a joyous life.

The Divine Holiness is the infinite intelligent spirit:

- I believe that He is the provider and source of all my needs.
- I want for nothing.
- Everything is provided for me according to divine order.
- My wealth flows in abundance.

Affirm these words above daily, and you will see changes in your life. As you do so, they would be imprinted in your subconscious mind. You will be encouraged and never be in distress of anything. Including good health, peace, harmony, and financial abundance, which is your prosperity.

Here is another affirmation below:

- The Lord is the infinite spirit. The source of all my supply.
- The Lord and I are one.
- The spirit of the Lord is in me. I shall want for nothing.
- The Lord's love flows through me in abundance.

Whilst you are affirming your needs, if any negative thought came up to mind, immediately cancel it with positive words. Keep saying the infinite spirit will guide your steps in all your ways, and all bills and needs will be met at this moment in time.

Always truly believe that your going out; and your coming in, will be well. Your faith in the Lord brings comfort to you, and all things good in health and wealth.

Manifesting with 'The Mirror Effect' Using these words in the sentences below are serious affirmation and it works:

- I am a child of the infinite spirit.
- I am made beautiful; and I am created wonderfully.
- I love myself, and I am at peace. Spirit which is God is in my heart.

- I will receive that which belongs to me according to divine order.
- Divine spirit fills my soul with love.
- The bill is being paid according to divine order.

You are not to worry about anything. You are affirming these because you are creating wealth for others, and for yourself because the infinite spirit lives within us all. All that you need will be for when you follow instructions according to divine order.

The spirit cannot prevent our riches but enables it. It lived in us, even that which is poorly. He makes everything well. All that we need will be multiplied. That is what the subconscious mind does. It multiplies and expands what the conscious mind sees and speaks out. The God and you are one. He made it so because the infinite dwells within you in your heart.

So, rejoice and be glad. Always say that which you truly believe in. The subconscious mind is a serious magnifier, as I mentioned earlier, and will elaborate your thoughts and your words, so be careful in what you wish for or speak out. Remember what the book of law and truth says:

- Whatsoever things are true.
- Whatsoever things are honest.
- Whatsoever things are just.
- Whatsoever things are pure.
- Whatsoever things are lovely.
- Whatsoever things are of good report; if there be any virtue, if there be any praise think on these things. *Philippians 4:8.*

So, engrave only the good thoughts about you and others. Declare and decree any bad negative thoughts to disappear in Jesus's name.

Call for divine riches, abundance of wealth, divine and spiritual abundance for all that which you request for yourself. This will bring riches of untold blessing in all that you do and need. You will in time experience success, joy, happiness, wealth, and infinite riches in blessing.

There will be new beginnings and openings, bringing multiplication of all that you wish for, so that you would be able to provide for others and for yourself.

Some of your blessings will come from people who are giving you things that you need. Others by good advice, direction on what course to take to your riches. The wise and richest man in Babylon. He gave advice to the interpreter such as:

- Act and stop procrastinating.
- Limit your spending.
- Make sure you save, by putting money aside.
- Look for opportunities that comes your way and go for it.
- Invest when you can, and you will see an exponential increase in your money.

We are to learn how to acquire riches.

Another way of manifesting:

- I saturate my mind. with the divine love that fills my heart.
- Divine spirit direct me in all ways.
- Divine intelligence strengthens me, and all those who inspires me, and I do business with.
- Divine spirit bless all of my customers.
- Divine peace and harmony fill my soul and theirs.

Recite this frequently as you can. Morning, afternoon, and evening. Shortly, you will experience openings showing up.

- Be anxious for nothing says the Bible.
- Do not worry.
- Cast every burden unto Jesus and go free.
- Be grateful for everything and give thanks for all what happened during the day before going to bed.
- Forgive yourself and forgive others too.

Then the subconscious mind goes to work on your wishes. It does not sleep. Know that it operates twenty-four hours a day.

I always say have a goal, a definite one and work towards that goal. It is your destination that you seek. By manifesting, you are planting a seed that will grow. Keep watering it with your meditation day and night, so it grows.

See what you want with your mind's eye from your imagination, and working towards your goal and achieving it. The infinite intelligent spirit is the divine Master. It takes care of our requests. Therefore, we are to change our mindset to change our life. Showing love always.

Sow the seed of love. Always keep love alive

in your heart.

- Love brings unity,
- Love restores faith, and
- Love heals all wounds.

You must believe in what you are affirming. Your thoughts become words. When you pray, recite this prayer boldly for your needs, such as these words:

- Infinite spirit, open the way for a home,
- My right partner,
- A friend by divine selection,
- Place me in the right position according to divine order.

It will always happen. Only believe and 'wait,' the key word is 'Patient.' I give thanks that all my needs are now manifesting in the right way by divine order.

The wonders of faith

This is where everything begins to fall into place; that which you have called for. The patience, and positive thinking had played a good part to this wonder of the Law of Attraction.

The divine gives us riches that is all around

us, and it is for us to discover them. Therefore, the riches forms part of the Life's Secrets. How we manifest the will of power to receive our wealth is important. You must remember that all what you say, will be effective and active in your life at some point. It depends when and how badly you need them. Therefore, always be positive. Use the following meditation to help you grow spiritually and achieve all what you require in your life:

- I and divine are one.
- Divine love fills my soul.
- Divine love let peace flows through me at all times,
- Divine spirit fills my mind in all ways. Let me be encouraged and lift up my spirit and strengthened me.
- Divine spirit gives me peace, harmony, joy, love, and understanding. Let my mind be filled with love at all times.

Affirmation for strength

❖ The joy of the Lord is my strength.

❖ I am expecting the best. My place on earth is to expect all good things.

❖ Peace and confidence be my strength.

Never be nervous in your journey towards your goal. If you do, you will not be able to achieve it. So, work with confidence. Know that your wish is to bless, inspire and dignify lives. Always say, 'I am beautiful and thankful that I am alive.' Recite this after your prayers:

'Let the words of my mouth; and the meditation of my heart be acceptable to you O Lord, my strength, and my redeemer.'

Patience: Patience is the key to achieving anything after manifesting. You should use the law of attraction to draw every good thing to you. Manifest that which you require for you and for others by divine inspiration.

THE SILENT LISTENER

The Bible says, 'Thou shalt also decree a thing, and it shall be established unto thee; and the light shall shine upon thy ways.' Job: 22:28. Whatsoever you ask for when you pray, believe that you have receive them and it will be so. You shall have them. Say it and believe.

CHAPTER 15

The Silent Listener

Remember the subconscious mind, this I call the *silent listener.* Whatever you say will register. As it registers your words, it goes to work on your request.

Remember to always use positive language as the silent listener cannot read what you meant to say. It acts on what it hears and what has been registered in the brain. You will have to choose the words you use carefully, to change your life. You should always use positive words as they bring forth good fruits.

One thing I want to clarify here, is the use of prayer and meditation. There are differences in the use of prayer and meditation. The Lord Jesus explains about prayers and praying in Matthew 6 in the Christian Bible. We are to pay great attention to his words. In this chapter he explains about prayers, faith, and our needs. I shall not attempt to explain the chapter here so as not to misled you or misinterpret the words, by reading into it the wrong way. The Bible is multi-facet, and anyone can interpret it in their way of understanding.

Please read the book of Matthew 6 to understand how to pray. It is our will to do what we are in this world for; and that is to live.

How we live is up to us to make it work as we have free will. So, do not go pass this chapter in Matthew. Read it through carefully with understanding for yourself. I advise you to read through the whole chapter, perhaps as many times as possible to get an understanding of what the message is saying.

Matthew 6. There are two verses in the chapter that I would like you to pay great attention to. Since I am dealing with the **Power of the mind, and Silent Listener,** it is important to look at what the verses say on prayer. Take note here:

Praying. 'But thou when thou prayest, enter into thy closet, and when thou hast shut thy door, pray to thy father which is in   secret;

and thy father which sees in secret shall reward thee openly.'

'But when ye pray, use not vain repetitions, as the heathen do: for they think that they shall be heard, for their much speaking.' *Matthew 6:7*.

Remember do not confuse *prayers with meditation.* Prayers does not need to be repeated, whilst meditation calls for constant repetition. We are being given the manner in which we are to pray. This appears in verses 9-13. Emphasis is placed on verse 12 and also an explanation to it. At this point, my advice is, before you kneel or stand to pray, ask for the forgiveness for yourself and for all those who wrong or hurt you, and those you have hurt. It is important for your peace of mind.

Remember the divine Lord will give attention to this area as expressed in verses 14 and 15. When you read **Matthew 6**, I would ask that you should take particular notice of what the verses of 22 to 31 says. Do not forget to put thoughts into what verse 33 is saying.

Many people always quote this verse in the

wrong context. Therefore, I would urge you to get understanding of this particular verse 33, which says: 'Seek ye first the kingdom of God, and his righteousness; and all these things shall be added unto you.' It is incumbent upon you to read the whole Chapter for better understanding and interpretation of the verses. Let me draw your attention now to meditation.

This is explained in the next chapter.

CHAPTER 16

Meditation

Meditation is different from praying. I would describe meditation as, the constant repetition of an affirmation. It should be done in a quiet place, the same as when praying you are to be in a quiet place so that you can concentrate. Note: Prayers does not need to be repeated over and over.

Keeping in concentration of that which you seek, to achieve over a period of time. No longer than five to ten minutes, done possibly in the morning and in the evenings. Let us say, if you would like to achieve good health, do the following: You would say: 'Heal me O Lord for thou art my healer.

Thank you, O Lord, that I am healed.' (5mins) Repeat this several times twice daily, for a week or more, and watch what happens.

The divine father knows what you are praying for and so it will be delivered in time according to your faith. The subconscious mind will print it in time and act on it. As it works 24 hours, it does not have a rest. It is actively working on your request even when you are sleeping. For this reason, it is advisable if you cannot sleep, you are to go to sleep with recorded meditation verses playing to help you fall asleep. As it calms the soul, so it heals the body during your sleep.

Some advice for the law of life.
I suggest that in order to survive in this universe, ask for knowledge, wisdom, and understanding. Always ask, and it shall be given to you; seek, and ye shall find; knock and it shall be opened unto you: For everyone that asketh receiveth, and he that seeketh findeth, and to him that knocketh, it shall be opened. *Matthew 7:7-8*

The gift of God is wisdom. To understand how the Law of Attraction works you must first *have enough faith to believe in the process which is the infinite spirit, which is the Creator.*

God is the spirit and the forever present in all life's processes, and the experiences that we undergo. It is the cause that affect that which is called for.

The Law of Opportunity

The *Law of Opportunity* will always appear whenever you try to invoke the *Law of Attraction.* The only way that it will not appear is that if you were not using the Law of Attraction to call for what you want. Information that I collected from using the Law of Attraction to create wealth met with negative setback as explained earlier in the book.

Everything under the sun came in the picture. There were request for money from several people, and other project appear, health was also a contributing factor to delay everything.

The project at hand.

People giving advice on what to do, and what not to do. All these were enough to trouble anyone, and to stop and ask question whether this Law of Attraction process is working. But this is the proof that it is working as many would want assurance.

However, the *Law of Attraction* requires patience. The **Law of Distraction** shows up to distract you from what you are calling upon for you and for others. When this distraction happens, that is when you need the *Law of Wisdom to discern what to do.*

Remember earlier on I talked about asking for knowledge and wisdom. The gift of wisdom gives discernment to help you figure out what to do. In order to deal with this distraction, you would have to go back to the point where you started the process, and call upon it again. You should never stop. The Law of Attraction does not need negativity.

You should always be positive when trying to invoke your wish. You should never be in doubt. You may be invoking a sum of money, or good health or a nice home. You should never think of where it will come from as the subconscious mind works like a miracle to bring forth your wish.

The 'Power of Will'

I have dealt with this earlier. It requires determination. The Law of the mind directs your thoughts to work for you and deliver. You are to know that the Lord will perfect that which concerns you. This is the truth from the Bible.

The infinite love will provide all your requirements.

You are to keep all things good and positive in your subconscious mind.

'Hard work with faith enables things to happen.' So, keep working on it. *Proverbs 12:11*

'Those who work their land will have abundant food, but those who chose fantasies have no sense.' *Philippians' 4:13* The Bible says:

'I can do all this through him who gives me strength.' Always do what you can to uplift others.

Do not contribute to the disablement of others.

When you work, tune in to the source within you, which is the energy to fill you up when you are drained. It is within you, 'the Will.'

There are times when there will be storms, in

all of our lives, alright! But do not lose hope, it will always pass. Tap into the source, it will work out. Be of service to people and always do the right thing. It is what you do that will last in a lifetime.

The good deed is what will last forever. In the end there will be peace in your heart knowing that you have done the right thing. Whatever you know is also a good thing.

One situation I know is a family of seventeen people. Their father had died and left a property of a town lot. Only three people lived in the property until the property fell into disrepair. So, one of the members who has the legal right to distribute the property wants to sell it so that every member could have a share of the proceeds. Given up her own property to boost the proceeds, and that is seen as a selfless act on the member.

Though people may not see it now, but later on it is the thought of the weak that matters, so that they may not be taken advantage of. This is the service that is expected from everyone to live life in this universe. It is not only to care for ourselves but, we are to think about others too.

The decision to sell the property was the right one, as the three people living in the property would want it for themselves, and leaving the fourteen others out.

We are given grace, which is the greatest gift of all in life, that enabled us to make contribution, and give thanks.

Knowing Life's secrets will enable us to live a perfect life.

Appreciation

Be grateful for everything.

1. Check your achievements, and if you appreciate it, give thanks, even if you do not, give thanks anyway.

2. Check out your life's journey and be thankful also.

3. Checkout what others have done for you, and what you have done for others, and give thanks.

4. Appreciate kindness, and be thankful.
5. Appreciate those who love on you, and be thankful.

6. Appreciate those who, and be thankful.

7. Appreciate the people in your life, and be thankful.

I hope that you will listen to others in silence, as it is one of the most important acts of true love. Showing that you are there for them.

Listening is what the Lord our Creator does all the time, and the father is a good listener too. Giving us time to vent, and say whatever is bothering us.

Warning!

Do not reveal your intentions to anyone until you achieve your dream goal. This is because, as soon as you reveal anything, you will be discouraged. Therefore, keep your ideas protected until you have seen your progress. If you do not listen to this advice, you will find out the hard way.

People are not seeing your ideas. It is not their vision, and therefore, they would be thinking that you are out of your senses for doing what you are doing. So, as your thoughts is being interfered with, you would want to drop your intentions as your mind has been affected by the thinking, and suggestions of others.

Another example of Law of Attraction: One afternoon, I spoke to my niece and sent her on an errand. Receiving the message, that a family member is seriously ill.

I gave instructions for her to be made available to him; and arrange medical attention.

Immediately, from then on, it became my responsibility.

Every month money is made available for his care, and so she also became the 'keeper of the find.' (She has to look after the sick man). When Lionel spoke to me on the phone, I could hardly hear his voice. Every word has to be interpreted. He was expressing his gratitude, saying thank you.

He asked for things he needed, and that which he wanted too. Food stuff, clothes; and moreover, there were other things that were important to him, amongst the list were things such as: radio, wheelchair, and so forth. Then I asked whether he was being fed; and about his pension, to know what they were doing with his pension?

He had retired as a government registrar. I figured out that Selma and I could at least help to make him comfortable. Better still buying more time for him to stay alive.

We joined forces together so we could support him, so that he gets better, at the most, to be able to carry out his own personal care. In the end it never happened, he died. My brother was one of the forgotten people, the isolated and hidden poor. Living like a pauper. When I figured this out, I was hurt badly, and felt angry at the other family members that he was living with inside the legacy, as they called the family land.

They were careless about his condition. He was in the midst of a family land that was not at all conducive to human living. He had a live-in partner who also did not care.

The only child of my brother was by the live-in partner; and she also did not care like her mother. They were supposed to be the primary carer for my brother. They failed him badly, and so did other family members. They could not help the sick, hungry, and the poor who were living under their nose.

We should all learn to help and care for our neighbours. That is what is required from us. This family failed him. It was evident that this man's days were numbered.

So, in late 2019, Lionel succumbed to his fate and died poor and hungry. How do we know he was hungry? At his final moment he called for porridge just before his last breath.

The doctors were baffled; and asked the questions that I had asked when I found out that he was ill. How long has this been going on?

The demise within a Legacy.

Does anyone deserve this? He called to him from afar, then walked a little, closer enough as he could, to hear a sound from the home, then moved more closer to see the end of a beautiful life. He then entered the compound. It was then it became clearer to him that not all would share of the legacy left by their father.

Another member attended. He peered through the window, as if it was something contagious, like a leper. Not seeing anything, and not wanting to enter, she moved a little closer and stood by the doorway and she said nothing and heard nothing. It was then she realized he had gone.

It was the end of a beautiful life. It was no secret, they all knew. He was not going to be part of the share of that legacy. He was going to die. Sharing here is part of the distraction that can occur whilst trying to work on Life's Secrets.

You will notice that at the end of your understanding, you would have learnt a lot more than you knew before. Nevertheless, the distraction kept on coming until it is time to produce the wonder.

This is your journey to manifesting recap here:

1. Do not be lazy.

2. Be persistent.

3. Be confident and courageous.

4. Have faith, and hope.

5. Have the right attitude.

6. Be reliable and honest.

Follow your heart.

Appreciate yourself more and associate yourself with the right people.

The Law of Attraction (LOA) brings joy of *enormous wonders*. So, discern and select the purpose of LOA.

I conclude, before you make a major decision. Pray and meditate on the issue. There is nothing wrong with doing this.

What is your ambition?

What have you been thinking about in your career path?

Your destiny awaits you, have you got an idea?

Working on your idea.

In your quest to deal with your idea of creating your wealth, you would have to believe in your idea, and command self-reliance.

Never accept the fate of poverty. Poverty is sickness. It is a disease that can ruin lives. It can kill.

Walk tall; and look forward to your riches coming to you as you work hard towards it. Having development growth needs sensible goals. You are to embrace the spirit of holiness in your life. Always listen to the voice of the spirit and not the voice of man.

What do you need goals for?

Take a look at your career. This is what you do with career if you want to be successful in life. Goals are important in life.

This book will help you with putting your idea into perspective, and bringing the reality alive. You would have read them along the way, and I hope you were taking notes. It will signpost you to your wealth, show you how to navigate your way to your own riches through the life secrets; and how to avoid pitfalls and unnecessary time-wasting ventures.

In this book there are five main truths of life's secrets on knowing the road map to wealth and riches to follow. Here they are below: Stop the poverty and uncertainty in life and embark on the understanding of Life's Secret.

Understanding Life's Secret.

You need wisdom and understanding. For

your benefit below are five areas to help us in our understanding:

Here are the ways of Understanding Life's Secrets

1. Money is God's wealth to help us live in abundance.

2. Spend money wisely and carefully, it is divine supply.

3. Meditate and manifest for your needs.

4. The riches we manifest and receive forms part of life's riches.

5. Look after your wealth to enable more to be added. It is our divine right to have all things good.

How to use your money wisely.

Money is sacred and it is resource and divine currency to help us live on earth. Below is listed 50 life's lessons that is taken from the book: 'I Cried – I know why I did.'

Some of Life's Hard Lessons below.

Fifty of life's hard lessons

1. Always listen to your parents.

2. As you grow older, listen carefully and pay great attention.

3. Note things down daily for future references.

4. Time passes by quickly. Take time to make wise choices.

5. Do not rush into any decision. Pray about it.

6. Put everything into prayers and wait.

7. Waiting is difficult, but yield the best fruit.

8. Enjoy every day as if it is your last. Enjoy your day, because that day is special, and never returns. It is gone for ever.

9. Friends and families are good.

10. When both leaves you, do not worry. It is not over yet. Friends and families, work out which one is best for you. When both leaves, perhaps, their work with you is complete.

11. When a family stop contact, know it is time to pull up your socks.

They may have done their job. Need not worry.

12.   Remember that the choices you made in life were caused by life's fate.

13.   Never worry too much when things do not go your way, or according to plan. It is meant to be life's lesson.

14.   If at first you don't succeed, try again. In life they say, we have three chances. Make sure you try harder next time.

15.   One of the best subjects' lesson in life is mathematics. I learnt some maths at school. Get your sums right, it will serve you till the end of your life.

16.   Continue learning maths for survival. When you go further at College, make sure you try out business studies.

17.   Another most

important thing in life is to love you. Yes, yourself.

18.   After loving yourself, you are able to love other people as required by

the law of nature, Love.

19.   Be attentive to what others are saying, and learn.

20.   Remember the advice to know your maths. Well, this is so that you will have knowledge of how money works in the world.

21.   I need to know about maths to know my sums. My additions, multiplications, Divisions and Subtraction, not forgetting my Equals to.

22.   Have respect for money know how it works in society, Batter is good also. Give and take. Exchange something for equal value, or better still more.

23.   Purchases = buying with cash or using credit cards. Exchange is not popular these days learn to buy with your own money and not with other people's money. If you save hard you are a genius. Save for what you want. Do not buy on impulse. Make a list and best of all 'Think.'

24.   Remember, if by any means you use people's money (i.e. credit card)

pay the whole sum before the month ends. If it is a loan, try as best as you can to avoid miss payments. The interests are very high. Use family member, friends or last resort Bank.

25.	When should we start saving? I can't say, but as early as possible. I started aged thirty-five.

26.	One of my good friends said to me, 'take out a private pension policy.' So I did without any question or doubt.

27.	Sometime in the 90s I needed money badly, and dipped into my pension pot for a loan without interest. It was good.

28.	Be aware that if you have a private pension, you can take a loan against it. Better than credit card, or bank loan; but pay it back quickly so you have the full benefit when you retire.

29.	To have respect for money, is to know fully how it operates.

30.	Making poor decisions is preparing to fail.

31.   Pray for the right life partner. One that will love the Lord more than you do.

32.   I thought I would never have to say this, but I need to. When you marry always have a separate bank account from your spouse. Have one joint community account. Your separate account is your security. There is so much evil in the world today. Very good people can switch by the evil of this world. Don't live to regret it.

33.   Sometimes there are odd situations. Not all those who say they love really loves.

34.   As a woman of Love, a prayer warrior and a believer, I have learnt a lot to get to where I am now.

35.   Note that not all your prayers will be answered ASAP (As soon as possible) sometimes we would have to wait.

36.   Waiting is of Love, and it is a good thing. Occasionally, we gets immediate miracle. We pray that our waiting will always be short.

37.   Have courage to continue your life's journey, when you make the inevitable mistakes or wrong turn. React with humility, dignity and bravery; then head on.

38.   Live one day at a time. Dress up and show up. You never know what that day brings.

39.   My philosophy in life now is: every day is a blessing, I dress up every day with my fine jewellery, as if I am going to a dinner date or some important function. I say, in case my Lord turns up at my door.

40.   Wake up with excitement, the best is yet to come.

41.   Live for now, free from debt. This is a blessing. I am a child of the universe. A 'god'. According to the word of Love. Life was breathed on me to give me life. That which is made by the hand of Love is god-child.

42.   What a blessing? There were times when I was the giver. Now, I sit and receive. That is the blessing of

Love.

43.   Now I want to thank Love for grace. It is sufficient for me. I have peace, and there is Love with me every day.

44.   Along life's journey, many stories were written. I have learnt a lot. Mistakes were many. Despite, I soldier on, until I reached the place where I am now.

45.   Money gives you freedom to live, and to make yourself happy. Life is sweet. So enjoy. I am enjoying the seed I sowed many, many years ago. It feels good collecting.

46.   Love you, love others and keep on the best side of Love. Don't forget to sow, ten percent tithe. It comes back ten-fold.

47.   Remember to forgive yourself, and others as and when possible. It is important for your sanity.

48.   Care deeply for human. Talk kindly to others, it does not mean they will be nice to you; but you have played

your part.

49.   Put your trust and faith in Love. Pray always and be the Princess or Prince of the King's daughter or son.

50.   In Life's Hard Lessons, we are all children of the universe. Respond to it with love and kindness. Pray for others when you pray. The angels and the Holy Spirit and Love will protect you.

When you follow these lessons above, it will make life easier and less complex. Whatever you do, save for what you want. If you can help it do not borrow. Above all, do not borrow to pay debt. If you do, you will be delving deeper and deeper into debt.

What you can do to clear your debt is to speak to the lender and explain your circumstances. Then work out a plan of how you can pay small amounts monthly or weekly. Remember hope is a wonderful thing. Have hope and faith and all things will work together for good.

Understanding

Remember that anything you do not understand you need to pray for revelation. I had said earlier to ask for discernment. This will open up your mind to know what to do in times of crisis or confusion.

Above all, have faith and hope. Keep this book beside you and read it again and again until you can understand where it is taking you.

Lastly, on these thoughts,

Always call for the higher power of anointing on your life, every blessed day.

The Author: Catherine Ashford, has a Post graduate Degree in Community Development. She is a retired Social Worker, and a Community Development Officer. A Diploma in Business Administration. Also, a Diploma in Beauty Therapy.

She has had many interesting careers behind her name. She had recently attained a Diploma in Organic Skincare Business whilst sheltering from the chaos of the world, in a COVID-19 stressed environment. She is a Christian Indi Author of Non-fiction and Fiction Titles. She is originally from Sierra Leone, West Africa and now resides in England, the United Kingdom. She is a Mentor and an Entrepreneur. She has written and published many Titles, and it is growing. She is a mother and grandmother.

NOTES

Don't forget to check out other titles. My forth-coming title:

Watch Out for!!!!!

' Maturity - The ABC of Ageing with Grace,'(non-fiction) and ' A Tale of Prince Agibu - and The Cursed Name' (fiction) . Will be coming Out

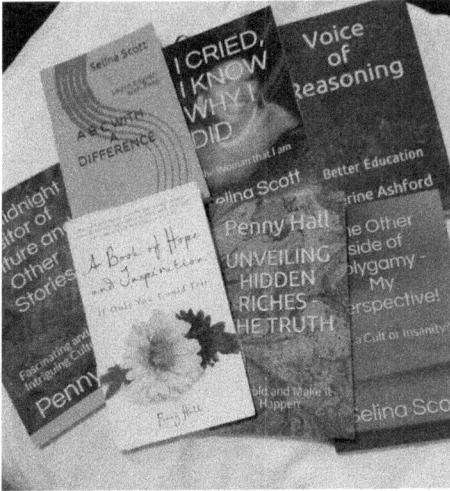

soon.

UNDERSTANDING LIFE'S SECRET

Q: **WHAT IS LIFE'S SECRET?**

Ans: Wisdom and Understanding. five areas to help us in our understanding Life's Secret:

1. Money is God's wealth to help us live in abundance.

2. Spend money wisely and carefully, it is divine supply.

3. Meditate and manifest for your needs.

4. The riches we manifest and receive forms part of life's riches.

5. Look after your wealth to enable more to be added. It is our divine right to have all things good.

Q: WHAT IS IT ABOUT?

Ans: It will signpost you to your wealth, show you how to navigate your way to your own riches through the life secrets; and how to avoid pitfalls and unnecessary time-wasting ventures.

Q: WHY IS THIS BOOK WRITTEN?

Ans: This book will help you with putting your idea into perspective, and bringing the reality alive.

Q: WHY SHOULD YOU READ THIS BOOK?

Ans: In your quest to deal with your idea

of creating your wealth, you would have to believe in your idea, and command self-reliance.

Q: HOW CAN YOU UNDERSTAND LIFE'S SECRET?

Ans: A good wisdom and understanding are needed to grasp the full principle of life. This should be a simple process which any one can grasp. To enable the principle of life to work in a perfect way, it requires understanding and discernment. You can only get this by asking for wisdom from the Divine infinite intelligence, which is the Holy Spirit. This enables the principle of life to manifest perfectly.

Q: HOW SHOULD YOU USE IT?

Ans: You are to Look at the key factors and information of the Law of Attraction and the Principles of Life.

www.ingramcontent.com/pod-product-compliance
Lightning Source LLC
Chambersburg PA
CBHW060041210326
41520CB00009B/1215

* 9 7 8 1 8 7 4 5 5 0 4 2 6 *